A STUDENT'S GUIDE TO CLASSICS

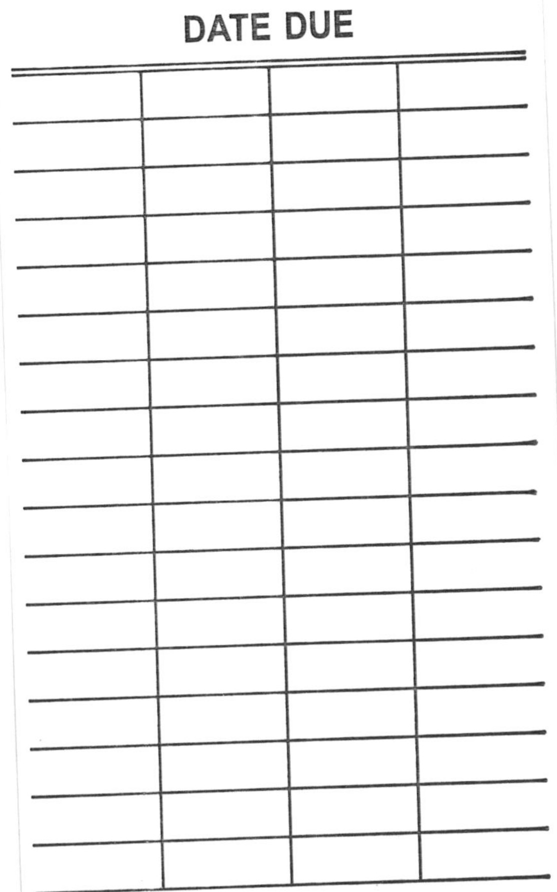

ISI GUIDES TO THE MAJOR DISCIPLINES

GENERAL EDITOR
JEFFREY O. NELSON

EDITOR
JEREMY M. BEER

PHILOSOPHY *Ralph M. McInerny*

LITERATURE *R. V. Young*

LIBERAL LEARNING *James V. Schall, S.J.*

HISTORY *John Lukacs*

CORE CURRICULUM *Mark C. Henrie*

U.S. HISTORY *Wilfred M. McClay*

ECONOMICS *Paul Heyne*

POLITICAL PHILOSOPHY *Harvey C. Mansfield*

PSYCHOLOGY *Daniel N. Robinson*

CLASSICS *Bruce S. Thornton*

A Student's Guide to Classics

Bruce S. Thornton

ISI Books
Wilmington, Delaware

A Student's Guide to Classics is made possible by grants from the Wilbur Foundation, the Lee and Ramona Bass Foundation, and the Huston Foundation. The Intercollegiate Studies Institute gratefully acknowledges their support.

Cataloging-in-Publication Data

Thornton, Bruce S.
A student's guide to the study of classics/ by
Bruce S. Thornton. —1st ed. —
Wilmington, Del. : ISI Books, c. 2003.

p; / cm.

ISBN: 1-932236-15-5 (pbk.)

1. Classical literature. 2. Classical education. 3. Humanities. 4. Social sciences. I. Title.

PA3013 .T46 2003 2003109729
88—dc22 CIP

ISI Books
Post Office Box 4431
Wilmington, DE 19807-0431

Cover design by Sam Torode
Manufactured in the United States

In memoriam
Evelyn Venable Mohr
Magistra carissima

CONTENTS

INTRODUCTION

Politics, philosophy, *history, epic, poetry, comedy, tragedy, rhetoric, democracy, aesthetics, science, liberty, senate, republic, judiciary, president, legislature*—the terms included in this brief but impressive list have two things in common: first, their referents constitute much of the political, intellectual, and cultural infrastructure of Western civilization; second, they all derive from ancient Greek and Latin.

Classics is the discipline that studies the language, literature, history, and civilizations of ancient Greece and Rome, two cultures that bequeathed to the West the greater part of its intellectual, political, and artistic heritage. For centuries Western education comprised the study of Greek and Latin and their surviving literary monuments. A familiarity with classics provided an understanding of the roots of Western culture, the key ideals, ideas, characters, stories, images, categories, and concepts that in turn made up a liberal education, or the training of the mind to exercise the independent, critical awareness necessary for a free citizen in a free republic.

Times of course have changed, and the study of Greek and Latin no longer occupies the central place it once held in the curriculum. Classics today is a small, shrinking university discipline kept alive, where it can be afforded, more because of prestige and tradition than because of a recognition of its central role in liberal education and in teaching the foundations of Western civilization. Yet at a time when Western civilization and its values are under assault, the need for classics is as urgent today as it was in the past. And people are still interested in antiquity: translations of classical texts continue to sell well, and popular films, *Gladiator* for instance, testify to an enduring fascination with the ancient Greeks and Romans. I hope that this brief introduction to classics will encourage students to study in more depth what Thomas Jefferson called a "sublime luxury," the ancient Greek and Latin languages and literatures.

WHAT IS CLASSICS?

THE DISCIPLINE of classics actually is made up of several different areas of study, all linked by a grounding in the

Greek and Latin languages, the study of which is called "philology." The first skill a classics student must learn is to read Greek and Latin, which means mastering their vocabulary, grammar, syntax, and morphology.[1] The study of these languages, moreover, usually proceeds through sentences adapted or taken whole from Greek and Roman authors.

Right from the start, then, classics students are learning about the great writers and works of antiquity, rather than learning how to ask for directions to the train station or the museum. Thus, even the technical study of Greek and Latin vocabulary and grammar exposes the student to some of the greatest literature, writers, and ideas in history. Here is an important difference between classics and other disciplines in the humanities: to a much greater degree classics teaches languages in a way that also introduces students to the culture, history, philosophy, and literature of Greece and Rome. But the first step remains learning the languages themselves, so that students eventually can read Greek and Latin masterpieces in their original languages.

After learning basic grammar, students begin to read ancient authors and decide in which specific area of classics they wish to concentrate. But no matter where students eventually focus, most will have first read a wide range of ancient texts in literature, history, and philosophy. This is another advantage of classics: since it is grounded in languages, students are compelled to become broadly educated in the whole culture of ancient Greece or Rome rather than just in some narrow subspecialty. Moreover, the habits of analysis and close reading required to understand the ancient languages often carry over into other areas, lessening (but not alas eliminating) the chance that students will be attracted to, or will themselves put forth, subjective or ideologically slanted interpretations. For in the end, no matter what ideological axe you want to grind, the Greek and Latin have to be accurately read and correctly translated, and this empirical, concrete procedure makes it difficult to get away with fuzzy or interested readings.

The possible areas of concentration in classics include the whole gamut of the humanities and social sciences: history (including religious, social, and intellectual history), philosophy, art (including vases, mosaics, and sculpture), architecture, literary criticism (including metrics and poetics), grammar, rhetoric, archaeology, geography, political science, and the histories of science, medicine, engineering, war, mathematics, and geometry. Moreover, classics is a fundamental discipline for those interested in the history of Christianity, the formation and transmission of the text of the New Testament, and the early Christian theologians and their doctrines (*patristics*).

In addition to these concentrations there are more technical foundational disciplines:

Epigraphy. This is the study of inscriptions engraved on stone, pottery, and sometimes wood (coins are the concern of *numismatics*). Thousands of inscriptions from the ancient world have survived, some intact, others badly mutilated. Once an inscription is discovered, the epigraphist must clean and decipher it. This process can be very difficult, not just because of the often-deteriorated condition of the stone but also because usually words are not separated and there are no small letters. Also, over time the style of some letters changes or letters pick up decorative flourishes. Inscriptions are valuable for historians of all sorts, whether social, political, religious, legal, or literary, since inscriptions cover a wide range of subject matter, from political decrees to expressions of affection for a dead spouse or child.

A fascinating example of epigraphical sleuthing involves the Colosseum in Rome. An inscription still visible today concerning repairs made in the fifth century A.D. is covered with holes in which were once anchored the metal letters of an earlier inscription. In 1995 Géza Alföldy of Heidelberg reconstructed the original inscription by analyzing the hole patterns. The reconstructed inscription dated to the time of the emperor Vespasian and specifically to the completion of a phase of construction of the Colosseum around A.D. 79. What we learn from this inscription is that the Colosseum was built "from the spoils" of a war; the only war that could have provided the necessary riches was the Jewish Revolt of A.D. 66–70, which ended with the destruction of the Temple and the removal of all its treasures. In other words, the plundered treasures of the Temple in Jerusalem financed the building of the Colosseum.[2]

Papyrology. Ancient writing was predominantly recorded on papyrus, a kind of paper made from a reed that grows mainly in Egypt. Papyrus deteriorates in damp climates, but the arid climes of Egypt and the Middle East, where many Greeks and then Romans lived for centuries, have allowed many papyrus documents to survive. Papyrology is the study of writing on papyrus and also fragments of pottery (*ostraca*) and wooden tablets, if discovered at the same site. Up to now about thirty thousand papyrus texts have been published, and many more remain in collections around the world. A papyrologist must decipher various styles of handwriting and then transcribe the writing, accounting for errors, misspellings, etc. A papyrus document is frequently damaged, with holes or torn-off sections, and so the text must be filled in with conjectures or simply left incomplete. Many great works of ancient Greek literature have survived only on papyrus. These include portions of several comedies by Menander, significant extracts from prose narratives, and philosophical works like the fourth-century B.C. *Constitution of Athens*—a discussion of Athenian government—along with numerous social documents such as letters, edicts, petitions, contracts, and receipts. Like epigraphists, papyrologists provide original sources for historians of literature, philosophy, politics, law, religion, and daily life.

A subdiscipline of papyrology is *paleography*, the study of how words and letters are written on papyrus. Paleography concerns the reading of ancient scripts and the history of their development and changes, which helps in dating documents, as well as the study of materials used in writing such as papyrus and inks.

Textual Criticism. Textual critics try to establish as correct a version of an ancient text as possible based on all surviving versions, including manuscripts, quotations in other authors, and fragments found on papyrus or ostraca. Most versions of ancient texts are the result of copies of copies over generations, and so errors by scribes frequently creep in. The modern textual critic must weigh all the surviving versions, determine which version is more reliable, reconstruct omissions, identify and correct scribal errors, and detect inconsistencies of authorial style, meter, or genre, all in an attempt to provide a text as close to the original as possible. The typical Greek or Latin text published today will provide at the bottom of each page a "critical apparatus," a list of all the variants and corrections ("emendations").

Knowledge of textual variants frequently is necessary when interpreting ancient literature. For example, a poem by the Roman poet Catullus (who is discussed below) is addressed to his friend Caelius and concerns a woman called Lesbia, with whom Catullus had a passionate affair but who now is seeing Caelius. In one variant of the text, he calls her "*our* Lesbia," which suggests that Caelius and Catullus are both seeing Lesbia. In the other variant, he calls her "*your* Lesbia," which implies that Catullus is through with her.

One's interpretation of this poem and the speaker's attitude to Lesbia will necessarily be influenced by which variant is followed.

It should be obvious that all these technical disciplines overlap somewhat and interconnect very closely. Most classicists have a basic knowledge of all these skills and will call on all or many of them when working with specific ancient texts or areas of research. Someone interested in the Colosseum, for example, will need to be knowledgeable about architecture, engineering, and epigraphy, but also will have to be familiar with the texts and manuscript traditions of works such as Martial's description of the opening games held in the Colosseum, or Suetonius's *Lives of the Caesars*. More importantly, however, the scholars doing this technical work provide the foundational material—especially the texts—upon which every classical scholar depends whether he or she is studying history, art, literary criticism, philosophy, or social history.

The primary experience of most people with the field of classics, however, will come with texts, the great surviving masterpieces that have influenced Western civilization for roughly twenty-five hundred years. And that experience in turn will most likely be with translations. Thus, the rest of this guide will focus on written texts, organized by genre. This approach means that whole important areas of ancient culture, particularly art and architecture, must regretfully be omitted. For more on ancient philosophy, the reader should consult Ralph M. McInerny's volume in this series.

A few other points should be kept in mind. First, while today we experience literature mostly by reading books silently by ourselves, in the ancient world literature was much more an oral and public experience. Thus, literature was necessarily social and political, rather than just a private taste or pastime. In other words, literature was taken much more seriously, its moral, political, and social implications more clearly accepted and recognized.

Second, we possess only a fraction of all the ancient Greek and Latin literature that once existed, and much of what we do have exists only in fragmentary form. To see how much has been lost, consider tragedy. We have thirty-three complete Greek plays from three playwrights. But in roughly a century of tragic performances (about 500–400 B.C.) there were probably a thousand plays produced, written by scores of poets. They exist now only as names and snippets of text, sometimes a mere few words long. Our generalizations about ancient literature, then, must always recognize that they apply in the main only to those works that have survived.

EPIC

THE EARLIEST SURVIVING literature of the West can be found in the two epics attributed to **Homer** (c. 750 B.C.) the *Iliad* and the *Odyssey*. A continuing scholarly question (the "Homeric question") centers on whether an actual person named Homer ever existed and composed the poems, or whether Homer is a fiction, the poems actually being a compilation from the oral epic tradition put together by several editors. Today most scholars attribute the poems to one or perhaps two authors.

The *Iliad* and the *Odyssey* are written in dactylic hexameters, a metrical pattern consisting of six feet of dactyls

---

HOMER (c. 750 B.C.) lived in the eighth century B.C., but we have very little reliable information about him. References in his poems suggest that he had knowledge of the eastern Aegean, and ancient testimony puts his home in Ionia, the Greek islands and cities on the coast of modern Turkey. The island of Chios or the city of Smyrna are his likeliest birthplaces. Everything else repeated about Homer—for example, that he was blind—is fanciful conjecture.

(a long syllable followed by two short ones) or spondees (two long syllables), with the fifth foot always a dactyl, and the sixth foot consisting of two syllables, the last either long or short. Originally epic was performed by a bard who had memorized thousands of traditional "formulae," whole lines or set phrases such as "long-haired Achaians [Greeks]" or "rosy-fingered dawn," which he then combined into a coherent story as he was performing. How old the oral epic tradition was by the time Homer composed his poems, whether Homer himself knew how to write or dictated to a scribe, and how much of his epics is traditional and how much invented by Homer himself are all fascinating but impossible-to-answer questions.

The subject matter of epic comprises the adventures, values, and experiences of aristocratic warriors who live in a world frequented by the gods, with whom they interact. Homer's epics are concerned with the period of the Trojan War and its aftermath (the hero's return home or *nostos*), i.e., the twelfth century B.C. In the modern era, archaeological discoveries have indeed confirmed that there once existed a civilization, called Mycenaean (after its most important ruins, discovered at Mycenae in central Greece) that resembled in many respects, particularly in its material culture, the world described by Homer. Yet thematically, Homer's epics reflect the period of the ninth to eighth century B.C., when the power of aristocratic clans was being challenged by the rise of the city-states and consensual governments.

The *Iliad*, the longer and probably the earlier of the two Homeric epics, covers a few weeks in the tenth year of the fighting at Troy. It focuses on the character of Achilles, the "best of the Achaians," who becomes enraged after a quarrel with Agamemnon, the leader of the Greek expedition and the brother of Menelaus, whose wife Helen ran off with the Trojan Paris and started the war. Homer traces the effects of Achilles' wrath, which include the death of his best friend Patroclus and the Trojan champion Hector, whose death at Achilles' hands signals the fall of Troy.

In the course of telling this story Homer brilliantly reveals the destructive effects of the aristocratic hero's code of honor and vengeance, which in the end sacrifices the community to the hero's personal quest for glory. Homer shows us that a political community cannot exist when ideals are based on personal honor achieved through violence, that our humanity depends on the "ties that bind," or our obligations to other humans, obligations that the hero, by contrast, will sacrifice to achieve glory.

The *Odyssey* tells of the hero Odysseus's adventures on his return home after the fall of Troy. It is a more accessible story than the *Iliad,* filled with fabulous locales, seductive temptresses, and fearsome monsters. But the *Odyssey* also movingly details the effects on the home front of a warrior's prolonged absence. Odysseus is a much more attractive character than the brooding, egocentric idealist Achilles. For one thing Odysseus is older, with a wife and son, and he displays a practical realism and an acceptance of those tragic limitations of life against which Achilles chafes.

Besides the wily Odysseus, the *Odyssey* contains several remarkable female characters, particularly Odysseus's wife Penelope, whose tricky ways are the equal of her husband's. The marriage of Penelope and Odysseus, based on similarities of character, virtues, and values, demonstrates the central role social institutions play in making human identity and a stable social order possible. The natural world is a harsh and dangerous place, but humans can flourish because they have minds like Odysseus's that can think up various contrivances that allow life to be successfully navigated, and also because they live in communities whose shared values, institutions, and codes lessen the destructive effects of nature's forces and our own equally destructive appetites and passions.

In both epics Homer describes an impressive depth and range of human behavior and motivation. He also recognizes the contradictions and complexities of the soul and the tragic limitations of human existence. Finally, Homer is a fabulous storyteller whose diction, similes, imagery, precise and vivid description of action, and economy of narrative are still fresh and entertaining after twenty-seven hundred years.

After Homer other epics were composed on various subjects, including the Trojan War and its origins, the wars fought over the city of Thebes by Oedipus's sons, and the return home of various Greek heroes. The collection of these stories is called the "Epic Cycle," and it has survived only in fragments and later summaries. In the third century A.D. **Quintus of Smyrna** (years of birth and death unknown) picked up where Homer left off in the *Iliad* to tell the story of Achilles' death, the Trojan horse, and the sack of Troy, among other adventures. Another important collection of hexameter poetry once attributed to Homer and written in the epic style comprises the "Homeric Hymns," which date from the eighth to the sixth centuries B.C. These are thirty-three poems of various lengths describing the adventures and attributes of the gods. The most interesting are the second, which tells the story of Demeter and her daughter Persephone, who is kidnapped by Hades, king of the underworld, and the fifth, which describes Aphrodite's liaison with the mortal Anchises.

Among the Greeks, Homer's literary and cultural authority was similar to that of Shakespeare among the English-speaking peoples—he was a master impossible to imitate. Yet in the early third century B.C. **Apollonius of Rhodes** (years of birth and death also unknown) published amidst much controversy the *Argonautica* (c. 270–45 B.C.), a hexameter poem about the voyage of Jason and the Argonauts in search of the Golden Fleece. The *Argonautica* is on one level a reworking of Homer, repeating many of epic's conventions and stylistic elements, such as the "extended simile," a detailed comparison that goes on for several lines. Yet at the same time the *Argonautica* reflects more contemporary (for Apollonius) concerns, such as the psychology of sexual passion, magic and fantasy, science and geography, and a learned interest in the origins of cult and ritual. Apollonius's self-consciousness about his poem's relationship to a venerated literary tradition is part of the work's appeal and interest.

The *Argonautica* was very popular among the Romans,

and its influence can be seen in the *Aeneid* of **Virgil** (70–19 B.C.). Before Virgil, the *Annales* (c. 169 B.C.) of **Ennius** (239–169 B.C.) had used Latin hexameters to portray Roman history as a Homeric epic, but only fragments of the *Annales* have survived (Ennius also was inspired by the traditional Roman practice of making a yearly public record of events, which was called the *annales maximi*). Virgil's *Aeneid*, however, was for centuries arguably the most influential work of classical literature in the West (Homer's epics were lost to Europe for centuries). The *Aeneid* tells the

---

Virgil (Publius Vergilius Maro, 70–19 B.C.) came from a village near Mantua and was educated in Milan, which suggests that his family was fairly wealthy. He lived for a while in Naples as a follower of the Greek philosopher Epicurus, who counseled retreat from the world into a community of like-minded friends. A long tradition has Virgil's father's land confiscated by Octavian and Marc Antony as part of a general proscription of land to pay off their legions in 40 B.C. But this biographical detail, along with the restoration of the land by Octavian, most likely derives from a crude biographical reading of the poet's first and ninth *Eclogues*, which mention the confiscations. Sometime after the *Eclogues* Virgil entered the circle of Maecenas, Octavian's friend who doled out largesse to poets. He quickly became one of the most celebrated (and richest) of Roman poets and was mentioned several times by other poets, including Horace, who praised his "tenderness and charm," and Propertius. Virgil was on his way to Greece when he caught a fever and died in Brundisium; his masterwork, the *Aeneid*, was nearly complete at the time (there is no evidence to support the story that he wanted his friends to burn the manuscript). He was buried in Naples.

story of "pious Aeneas," the Trojan who flees the fall of Troy to found the city of Rome, experiencing along the way Odyssean adventures and then having to fight Iliadic battles with the Latins once he reaches Italy. But the *Aeneid* is much more than just a Romanization of Homer.

Combining the Ennean tradition of epic history with a complex literary conversation with Homer, Apollonius of Rhodes, and Greek tragedians like Euripides, Virgil created a masterpiece that examines the possibilities of order on the divine, natural, psychological, artistic, ethical, and political levels. No mere propagandist for the emperor Augustus and no mere imitator of Homer, as he is often mischaracterized, Virgil recognizes the necessity of order, including the political, yet at the same time he acknowledges the terrible price that often must be paid to achieve that order. He sees a cosmos riven from top to bottom by the intimate interplay of order and chaos, a vast conflict in which struggling mortals have a role to play and a burden to bear, often at great personal cost. This combination of optimism and pessimism, hope and despair, idealism and grim realism gives the *Aeneid* its distinct character. At the same time, the *Aeneid* is a virtuoso performance of poetic skill and craft at every level, from its memorable characters and vivid descriptions to its chiseled lines that for a thousand years were the common cultural possessions of every educated person.

Another influential Latin work usually classified as an epic, since it is written in dactylic hexameters, is the *Metamorphoses* (c. A.D. 8) of **Ovid** (43 B.C.–A.D. 17). But the twelve books of Ovid's poem do not address the usual epic subjects of warrior heroism and battle. Instead, starting with the creation of the world and ending with Julius Caesar's transformation into a god, Ovid intricately interlocks scores of short tales whose common thread is change of bodily form. Well-known stories include that of the famous singer

---

Ovid (Publius Ovidius Naso, 43 B.C.–A.D. 17) came from the Abruzzi, or the "heel" of Italy. His father was descended from an old equestrian or "knightly" family. Ovid went to Rome for his education and toured Greece, as was usual for a young man of his social class. After some minor posts in the judiciary, he devoted his life to poetry. At the height of his fame Augustus banished him from Rome to the dreary Black Sea city of Tomis. Ovid mentions two "offenses" that led to his exile: a "poem" and a "mistake." The poem is his "Art of Love," a witty parody of advice manuals on how to carry on an adulterous affair, the sort of thing that countered Augustus's attempt to restore the old Roman morality. As for the mistake, it probably involved some scandal, inadvertently witnessed by Ovid, that concerned the royal house: the poet refers to the myth of Actaeon, a hunter who accidentally saw the virgin goddess Diana naked and was torn apart by his own dogs. Ovid died in Tomis, leaving behind a daughter and two grandchildren as well as his wife, who had stayed in Rome.

Orpheus and his bride Eurydice, whom the singer descends into Hell to rescue, and Arachne, who challenged the goddess Minerva to a weaving contest and ended up being turned into a spider. Along the way Ovid self-consciously engages a wide range of Greek and Roman writing and myth, telling his tales with a keen eye for narrative and visual detail that anticipates at times the realist novel. The *Metamorphoses* was an important influence on Renaissance literature, its tales providing the subjects for numerous paintings, sculptures, and literary works. Shakespeare knew it in Arthur Golding's translation.

After Virgil no epics survive that reach the level of poetic and philosophical sophistication of the *Aeneid*. **Statius**'s (first century A.D.) *Thebaid*, about the war between Oedipus's sons for the rule of Thebes, was popular in the Middle Ages and the Renaissance, no doubt partly because of a tradition that Saint Paul had converted Statius to Christianity. Another influential epic was the *Bellum civile* or *Pharsalia* (*The Civil War*) of **Lucan** (A.D. 39–65), which detailed in epic style the destruction of the Roman Republic and the loss of freedom that followed the wars between Julius Caesar and Pompey in 48 B.C. In the eighteenth century Lucan was a favorite of champions of republicanism, particularly for his portrait of Cato of Utica (95–46 B.C.). Cato committed suicide rather than submit to Caesar, and so became the emblem of the principled republican who prefers freedom to tyranny.

POETRY

A RICH VARIETY of poetry has survived from ancient Greece and Rome, spanning over a thousand years and a wide range of genres and meters. One of the oldest kinds is **didactic** poetry, or poetry that teaches. **Hesiod** (c. 700 B.C.) is often categorized as an epic poet, since he writes in the hexameters and style of Homer. His subject matter, however, is very different.

Hesiod's *Theogony* describes the creation of the cosmos and the birth and genealogies of the gods; especially important is the story of Prometheus, who steals fire from heaven

---

HESIOD (c. 700 B.C.) was a near contemporary of Homer. His poems give us some biographical information: that his father gave up being a merchant and moved to Boeotia, the region northwest of Athens; that he once won a tripod in a singing contest; and that he was swindled by his brother Perses, with the collusion of local aristocrats, out of part of his inheritance. His poems suggest that he held the values and worldview of the small farmer who distrusts equally the city and the nobility.

and saves the race of mortals from extinction. The *Works and Days*, also written in hexameters, is a hodgepodge of maxims, proverbs, fables, parables, and myths. A moral treatise on the importance of hard work and the dangers of idleness, the poem is addressed to the poet's brother Persis, who apparently cheated Hesiod out of some of his inheritance and then squandered it. In addition, the *Works and Days* contains much practical knowledge concerning farming and sailing, with an almanac of lucky and unlucky days. Particularly noteworthy are the myth of Pandora, the first woman (whose curiosity unleashes evil on mankind); another version of the Prometheus story; and the myth of the Five Ages, which starts with a paradisiacal Golden Age and then degenerates into the wicked present, the Iron Age of suffering, hard work, disease, and moral decay.

Moral and philosophical instruction remained an important topic of didactic poetry after Hesiod. Philosophers such as **Empedocles** (c. 492–432 B.C.) and **Parmenides** (c. 450 B.C.) set out their ideas in poems that addressed issues such as how the world works (physics), the nature of existence or being (ontology), and the means of gaining knowledge (epistemology). Later during the Hellenistic period (c. 300–100 B.C.) more specialized topics turn up in didactic poetry, such as **Nicander**'s (c. 130 B.C.) work on snakes, spiders, and poisonous insects (*Theriaca*), his treatise on poisons (*Alexipharmaca*), and **Aratus**'s (c. 315 B.C.–c. 240 B.C.) *Phaenomena*, which concerns the constellations. The *Phaenomena* was very popular in the ancient world and was translated into Arabic.

The **lyric** genre of poetry comprised poems that were sung to the accompaniment of a lyre; this poetry is sometimes called *melic*, from the Greek word for "song." The solo performance of lyric was called *monody*, in contrast to choral songs performed by a group of singers who also danced in costume. The earliest lyric poetry dates to the seventh century B.C., and even in fragmentary form the influence of Homer is evident in its imagery and phrasing. In subject matter, however, lyric frequently focuses on the personal experiences of the poet, illustrated with traditional myths and covering themes such as love, politics, war, friendship, drinking, and settling scores with enemies.

Many names of lyric poets survive but most of their poems have done so only in fragments. Two important monodic poets came from the island of Lesbos. **Alcaeus** (born c. 625–620 B.C.) in his surviving fragments writes about friendship, the political struggles on Lesbos against various tyrants, exile, shipwreck, and drinking, all developed with vigorous descriptions and mythic exemplars. It is in Alcaeus that we find the earliest use of the "ship of state" metaphor. More influential has been **Sappho** (born c. 650 B.C.), known in ancient times as the "tenth muse." Only two of her complete poems survive, along with numerous fragments, but in them we see a wide variety of subjects, including Sappho's brother and daughter, poetry, beauty, marriage, hymns to gods, myth, and political struggles on Lesbos. Sappho is most famous for her poems describing her powerful sexual attraction to girls, in which her emotions are vividly rendered with striking imagery, yet always poetically controlled. The musical beauty of her poetry was famous in antiquity.

Choral lyric poetry was usually part of a public ritual or

SAPPHO (born c. 650 B.C.) was born on Lesbos, an island near the coast of modern-day northern Turkey, in the second half of the seventh century B.C. Imaginary biographical details about Sappho began circulating even in antiquity—that she was a lesbian, a prostitute, short and ugly, ran a finishing school for aristocratic girls, and threw herself off a cliff over unrequited love for a ferryman. It is more certain that as a member of an aristocratic clan she was involved in the political struggles on Lesbos, which led to exile for a while in Sicily. Based on the fragments of her poetry (one complete poem out of nine papyrus-roll books survive), she had a husband, a daughter named Cleis, and a brother who apparently squandered money on a courtesan.

celebration. Examples include hymns to gods, including the "paean" for Apollo and the "dithyramb" for Dionysus, the maiden-song (*partheneion*), sung by a chorus of girls, and the wedding-song (*hymenaios*), among others. By the sixth century B.C. secular subjects appear in choral lyric: "panegyrics" to rulers and aristocrats who were the poets' patrons, and "victory odes" (*epinicia*) commissioned by aristocratic victors in public games such as the Olympics. These choral songs, often performed at competitions, were composed in elaborate metrical patterns and linked the occasion or subject to more generalized human experience. A mythic narrative usually served as the centerpiece of the song.

Two choral poets particularly noteworthy are **Simonides** (born c. 556 B.C.) and **Pindar** (c. 518–430 B.C.). Simonides composed, among many other genres of poems, victory odes and dithyrambs, the latter winning some fifty-seven competitions. Unfortunately, none of these poems survive intact. With Pindar, however, we have forty-five victory odes commissioned by winners in the four Panhellenic athletic festivals celebrated at Olympia, Delphi (the Pythian Games), Nemea, and Corinth (the Isthmian Games); however, he composed poems in nearly every type of choral song. His victory odes are very elaborate, complex, highly stylized celebratory descriptions of the athlete's achievement, with flattering references to his aristocratic clan and a mythic narrative usually linked to the athlete's family or city. The athlete's experience is set in the context of a more general view of human life and moral instruction.

Another influential genre of poetry is called **elegiac**, after the meter of the same name. This metrical pattern consists of couplets that alternate a dactylic hexameter line with a second made up of a dactylic pentameter. Elegiac poetry covers a wide range of subjects and lengths; its use in funeral laments and epitaphs gives us our modern somber meaning of the word elegiac.

The Athenian politician **Solon** (died c. 560 B.C.), whose reforms of the Athenian constitution were important developments in creating Athenian democracy, wrote elegiac poems explaining and defending his political reforms. **Archilochus** (active c. 650 B.C.) treated many of the same subjects as the lyric poets—friendship, love, politics, and war. One of his most famous poems describes how he threw away his shield during a battle and ran away. "I can buy another just as good," he shrugs. The largest collection of elegy comprises the fourteen hundred lines attributed to **Theognis** (active c. 550–540 B.C.). Theognis was an old aristocrat displeased at the new status and power of men who "once lived like deer" but now think that their wealth makes them as good as the aristocracy. Theognis's poems are also filled with moral, practical, or ethical advice for his young friend (or lover) Cyrnus. By the fifth century B.C. the elegy was a form of poetry particularly associated with "symposia" or drinking parties at which the guests would recite verse and hold philosophical discussions (as in Plato's dialogue, the *Symposium*). Thus, many elegies take as their subjects drinking and love.

The **epigram** is another important poetic genre, one that is sometimes confused with elegy because epigrams were also written in elegiac couplets. Originally epigrams were written as inscriptions on objects such as tombs, and many early epigrams are anonymous. An early writer associated with epigrams is Simonides, whom we've already met as an elegist. Although there is some doubt that he actually wrote them, his epigrams about the Persian Wars (490 and 480/79 B.C.) are the most famous, especially the one commending the three hundred Spartans massacred at Thermopylae: "Go tell the Spartans, stranger, that we lie here dead, obedient to their commands."

By the Hellenistic period—the term we use to describe

Greek culture from the death of Alexander the Great (323 B.C.) to the dominance of Rome (30 B.C.)— epigrams were composed more often as literature rather than as inscriptions and covered a wide variety of topics, including fictitious dedications to everyday people like hunters or prostitutes, funeral laments for dead pets, and the usual topics of politics, family, friends, drinking, love, and sex. In this period the epigram becomes highly stylized and self-conscious while still retaining its emphasis on brevity and wit. Two Hellenistic writers of epigrams worth noting are **Asclepiades** (c. 300–279 B.C.), whose repertoire of imagery describing the effects of sexual passion has influenced all subsequent love poetry; and **Callimachus** (born c. 310 B.C.), who supposedly wrote more than eight hundred books in a wide variety of genres, including hymns to gods (which have survived). Sixty-four of his epigrams are extant, perhaps the most beautiful being his moving epigram about his dead friend Heraclitus.

Most Greek poets wrote in various genres, and in the Hellenistic period poets were conscious of several centuries of predecessors. They were not content to remain restricted by generic categories or strictures and so self-consciously experimented with various forms and subject matters, challenging the tradition at the same time they paid it homage. Callimachus's *Aetia (Origins)*, of whose four thousand lines only a handful and some fragments have survived, used the elegiac form to present a wide range of literary subjects, from long epigrams about tombs and statues to narratives on mythic tales, all knit together by an antiquarian interest in "origins." Another Hellenistic poet, **Theocritus** (active c. 270 B.C.), composed, in addition to twenty-four epigrams, *Idylls*, which in Greek means something like "vignettes." These are highly finished, poetically complex depictions of "slice-of-life" scenes ranging from shepherds in Sicily to middle-class housewives in Alexandria. His so-called bucolic idylls, those describing rural life in Sicily, initiate the long-lived pastoral tradition in Western literature, which uses the life of shepherds as a metaphor for exploring love and art, leisure and freedom, politics and nature. Finally, both Callimachus and Theocritus display a creative and innovative self-consciousness about the craft of poetry that was an important influence on Roman poets.

This brief survey discusses a mere fraction of the poetry and poets who wrote over several centuries of Greek history. Unfortunately, most have survived only in fragmentary form. But enough has come down to us intact to reveal a remarkable tradition of poetic craftsmanship in a wide variety of metrical patterns, subject matter, and genres, a tradition that shaped and enriched the literature of the West.

Roman poetry was the first beneficiary of this priceless heritage. Roman poets were intimately familiar with the several centuries of Greek poetry that had preceded them, as well as with the Greek scholarship on poetry produced in the Hellenistic period. Much of the work of the early Roman innovators of the late second and early first centuries B.C. is lost or has survived only in fragments. However, we do know that these poets embraced Hellenistic Greek literature as models, and by the early first century were known as *neoterics* or "new poets."

Two of the greatest works of Roman literature are **didactic** poems. *On the Nature of Things,* by **Lucretius** (c. 95–55 B.C.), is an explication of the philosophy of Epicurus (341–270 B.C.). Epicurus taught that all reality is material, mere atoms in random motion; that the soul dies with the body and that the gods are indifferent to human behavior; and that the greatest good is the pleasure of the soul freed from anxiety and pain. Lucretius expounds Epicurus's thoughts in hexameter lines filled with remarkable imagery and set pieces such as the description of the sacrifice of

Iphigenia by Agamemnon, which Lucretius concludes with the line that would become one of the Enlightenment's rallying cries: "Such great evils Religion has made acceptable!"

An even greater poem, though one owing much to Lucretius, is Virgil's *Georgics* (c. 29 B.C.), a brilliant meditation on the possibilities of human order in a harsh natural world. Farming had been the subject of other didactic works, including the *Re Rustica* (37 B.C.) of **Varro** (116–27 B.C.), written in dialogue form, and the prose treatise *De Agri Cultura* of **Cato the Elder** (234–149 B.C.). But Virgil uses agriculture as a controlling metaphor for discussing man's relationship to the natural world and the gods, and for exploring the connection between the values of political order and those of farming. The modulation between optimism about man's ability to create order and pessimism over the disorder caused by his passions and appetites is as effective here for Virgil as it would be later in the *Aeneid.* The *Georgics*'s exploration of the links between farming and political order was an important precursor to eighteenth- and nineteenth-century agrarianism, particularly the agrarian social philosophy embraced by a good many of the American founders.

After Virgil the best didactic poems in Latin are actually parodies, Ovid's *Art of Love* and *Remedies for Love.* The first of these gives somewhat tongue-in-cheek instruction in how to court a mistress and carry on an illicit affair, replete with illustrations from myth and vivid observations of the Roman social scene. In a similar style, the *Remedies* advises its readers how to get out of an affair. Another didactic work of Ovid is the *Fasti* or *Calendar*, which devotes one book to each month of the Roman calendar and its religious celebrations (only the first six books survive).

The early innovators of Latin **lyric** are lost or survive only in fragments. However, we do have 114 poems by **Catullus** (c. 84–54 B.C.) in a wide variety of meters and subject matters, including epigrams, hymns, a narrative mini-epic, and elegies on his love affair with a married woman he calls Lesbia. In these latter poems we see an important advance beyond the usually light-hearted treatment of sexual desire found in the Hellenistic poets. Catullus delves into the complexities and contradictions of illicit desire, the way it can divide the soul between duty and passion, pleasure and shame. Yet like his poetic mentor Sappho, Catullus always maintains the most rigorous poetic control over his subject, even when meticulously documenting the hysterical hatred and lust aroused by the shameless Lesbia.

Indeed, in order to attain the scope necessary for such psychological analysis Catullus expanded the epigram into a new genre, sometimes called the "subjective-erotic elegy," so called because these poems are written in elegiac couplets and focus on the impact of sexual desire on the poet's consciousness. Poets in this genre whose works have survived include **Propertius** (c. 50–c. 2 B.C.), **Tibullus** (c. 55–19 B.C.), and Ovid. Propertius's love poems concern his affair with a woman whom he calls Cynthia. They elaborate, with numerous mythological examples and sometimes complex allusions, the experience of illicit love into a full-time career that displaces the traditional Roman "course of honors" in politics and the military. The last two books of the collection treat a wider variety of subject matter, including poems on "origins" in the manner of Callimachus. Like Propertius, Tibullus is a "soldier" of love and the "slave" of his mistress Delia, and he documents the mundane details and psychological impact of this erotic soldiering and slavery. Finally, in Ovid's *Amores* we see the motifs of love elegy hardening into highly polished, ironic, witty conventions that lack the contradictions, doubts, and anxiety over the way illicit love challenges traditional Roman family values, a tension that makes the earlier poets' work more dramatic.

Two more lyric poets tower over the corpus of Roman poetry—Virgil and Horace. Virgil's first poetic work is the *Eclogues* or "Selections." These poems, often called "pastorals," are written in dactylic hexameter and take as their theme the rural milieu of farmers and shepherds explored in Theocritus's *Idylls*. Theocritus's imagined rural world of flowers and trees and streams, however, seems timeless and removed from the power of politics and the state. In contrast, Virgil's *locus amoenus,* or "pleasant spot," exists in the shadow of Roman political power and amidst the pressure of historical change that challenges the autonomy, freedom, leisure, and creativity of pastoral life. This conflict is seen in the first lines of the first *Eclogue*, which describe the shepherd Tityrus "reclining in the shade" while Meliboeus, his land appropriated for a Roman soldier, must go off into exile. So influential were the *Eclogues*, especially the first, on subsequent Western literature that literary historian E. R. Curtius once asserted that "[a]nyone unfamiliar with that short poem lacks one key to the literary tradition of Europe."[3]

Next to Virgil, the Roman poet who influenced European poetry the most is **Horace** (65–8 B.C.). A huge body of Horace's work in several different genres has survived, including four books of *Odes* that self-consciously imitate earlier Greek lyric models, especially Alcaeus. Horace's poems cover the whole gamut of themes treated in earlier lyric—love, drinking, friendship, politics—and include a famous poem celebrating the death of Cleopatra. But Horace's poems are developed in the complex and sophisticated style of Hellenistic poetry, and as such are filled with learned allusions to other poetry, geography, and myth. Many of the poems also express philosophical advice about how to live, containing memorable statements concerning the brevity of life and the importance of enjoying each day. For centuries phrases from Horace's poems were an essential part of every learned person's education. The praise of moderation Horace calls the "golden mean" (*auream mediocritam*); the

---

HORACE (QUINTUS HORATIUS FLACCUS, 65–8 B.C.) was born in Apulia in southeastern Italy. He was the son of a freedman (that is, an ex-slave, though probably an Italian) who was a small farmer and auctioneer. Horace's father must have done well, for he sent Horace to Rome and then Athens, where he met Brutus, the assassin of Caesar. Horace fought on the side of Brutus in the war against Octavian and Antony. Though his family lost their land after the defeat of Brutus, Horace was allowed to return to Italy, where he became a salaried government official, began to write poetry, and met Virgil, who recommended him to Maecenas (38 B.C.). Maecenas gave Horace a farm in the Sabine country northeast of Rome, which provided the poet with the leisure and financial independence to write poetry.

rightness of dying for one's country (*Dulce et decorum est pro patria mori*); and the need to enjoy life expressed in the dictum to "seize the day" (*carpe diem*) all come from Horace's *Odes*.

Horace represents the high point of Latin lyric. After him, some lyric poems appear in other kinds of writing, and fragments and names of lyric poets survive, but the genre will not become vital again until Christian poets take it up.

The earliest Latin **epigrams** were usually written for the tombs of famous persons, such as Ennius's second-century B.C. epigrams on the tomb of Scipio Africanus,

---

CATULLUS, GAIUS VALERIUS (C. 84–C. 54 B.C.) was born into a prominent family near Verona but lived most of his life in Rome. If his poems can be trusted, he was on the staff of a provincial governor in Bithynia, in modern Turkey, in 57–56; it was probably on his journey there that he visited the grave of his brother near Troy. He seems to have been an opponent of Caesar, but then he later accepted Caesar's friendship. Evidence suggests that Catullus was part of a social and artistic movement that rejected the ideas of Roman culture for the values of Hellenistic Greek civilization, which focused on the individual and his sensibility and experiences rather than on his duty to the state. If his poetry is an accurate reflection of his life, then Catullus was involved in a passionate affair with a rich aristocratic woman, most likely Clodia Pulcher Metellus, the wife of a consul. He apparently died young. As with Sappho, many fanciful biographical details about Catullus's life have been extrapolated from his poetry.

the Roman who defeated Hannibal at the Battle of Zama in 202 B.C. Only a handful of epigrams not written as epitaphs survive from the period preceding Catullus, though numerous fragments and references in other authors suggest that the genre was popular. In Catullus we find epigrams on love, politics, friendship, the composition of poetry, revenge on enemies, and a particularly moving epigram about the poet's visit to the tomb of his brother. In Catullus's hands, epigrams arising from the poet's everyday experiences transcend the merely witty detailing of trivia sometimes found in Greek epigram to become highly finished, complex works of art.

After Catullus the most important surviving Roman writer of epigrams is **Martial** (c. A.D. 40–104), who was born in Spain but lived most of his life in Rome. Some of Martial's epigrams are typical of Greek models, including epitaphs and occasional poems on various events. But most of his epigrams follow the model of Catullus both in meter and in the literary sophistication brought to the genre's usual topics. In Martial's hands the mundane details of everyday life and the passing scene are presented with social and psychological realism and biting wit. So acute are Martial's powers of observation that even after twenty centuries we can recognize in his poems the perennial foibles, contradictions, and absurdities of human nature. Martial is perhaps most famous for his endings, which often surprise the reader with some unanticipated point or twist, as in the following epigram about a doctor turned undertaker: "What he does as an undertaker, he had done as a doctor"—that is, he continues to bury his customers.

Satire is a poetic genre the subject matter of which is similar to that of some epigrams. According to the Roman rhetorician **Quintilian** (c. A.D. 35–90.), satire is a Roman invention. Like the Latin word for a dish full of a variety of foods from which it derives, satire treats a wide variety of

---

MARTIAL (MARCUS VALERIUS MARTIALIS, c. a.d. 40–c. 104) was one of an influential group of Spaniards, also including Seneca the Younger and Quintilian, who were active in Rome in the first century. In Rome, Martial sought patronage from the emperor Domitian and wrote panegyrics for other powerful patrons. His reputation led to his being given a commission to celebrate in verse the opening of the Colosseum in 80, and he was awarded the *ius trium liberorum*, an honor started by Augustus to recognize parents by giving them certain exemptions, such as from being a guardian, which could be expensive. Martial, a friend of many of the most influential people of his day, wrote imperial propaganda—although he complains that he didn't make much money doing so. He was the most popular writer of his time, read even in the provinces. After the death of Domitian, however, his star fell. He returned to Spain in 98, where he lived on a small farm given him by a wealthy widow. He died in Spain sometime between 101 and 104.

subjects in an equally diverse variety of styles and authorial roles. But the essential element of all satire is an attack on hypocrisy and pretension delivered with brutal wit and driven by the imperative "to tell the truth while laughing," as the great Roman satirist Horace put it.

Despite its Roman origins, satire does have precursors in Greek literature. The motif of the author abusing the corruption of his society or the vices of his enemies appears in a type of Greek poem called "iambics," after one of the meters in which these poems were composed. Horace's *Epodes* (c. 30 B.C.) used the meters of iambics for the first time in Roman poetry, but not all of these poems employ invective to attack social and moral corruption. Another influence on Roman satire was the "diatribe," which purported to be a transcript of a public lecture given by a philosopher who used jokes, everyday language, and even vulgarity to attack vice and make a moral point. The Cynic philosopher **Menippus** (active c. 300–250 B.C.) gave his name to a style of satire that mixed verse and prose. The *Satyricon* of Petronius (see below) incorporated Menippean satires in its exposure of the *nouveau riche* vulgarity of imperial Rome.

All of these Greek influences can be found in the satirists writing before Horace, but unfortunately only lines and fragments of these earlier satirists survive. Horace's eighteen *Satires* (c. 30 B.C.), which he called *Sermones* or "conversations" in reference to their colloquial style and fluid shifts from subject to subject, are the most substantial examples of the genre from the late Republic. In these conversations Horace uses his own life and experiences, as well as the vices of others, to exhort his readers to moral improvement. Compared to the fragments of his model **Lucilius** (born c. 180 B.C.), Horace is more restrained and cautious in his choice of targets, perhaps reflecting the political uncertainty of the dying Republic and then, later, the character of Augustus's rule. Thus Horace tends to focus his satire on types rather than real people. One famous *Satire* retells the fable of the city mouse and the country mouse in order to chastise the excessive luxury and sensuality of the Roman ruling class.

In the sixteen satires of **Juvenal** (c. A.D. 60–130) the angry chastisement of vice and folly returns, though his later satires are more restrained and detached. Moreover, Juvenal's poems prefer the grand style of epic and tragedy to the coarseness of Lucilius or the conversational urbanity of Horace. Juvenal's topics include everything that to him typified the corruption of Rome: the decadence of the ruling class and patrons, sycophantic clients, promiscuous homosexuals, greed, social climbers, foreigners, the emperor and his toadying courtiers, effeminate men, loose wives. Particularly famous are the third satire, describing the miseries of living in Rome, and the tenth, a meditation on the insignificance of human achievement in the face of devouring time. Samuel Johnson composed imitations of both these poems. Juvenal's tone of "savage indignation"—as W. B. Yeats described Jonathon Swift's satire—has had a long influence on Western satiric literature, and his poems have generated numerous famous quotations, including "A sound mind in a sound body" (*mens sana in corpore sano*) and "Who will guard the guardians?" (*Quis custodiet ipsos custodes?*)

One last poetic genre that should be mentioned is the verse letter or **epistle**. This seems to be a wholly Roman invention, apart from a few Hellenistic poems that make an invitation in the form of a letter. Some fragments of epistles by Lucilius have survived, and a few poems of Catullus are cast as letters. Horace's *Epistles* (c. 20 B.C.) are the earliest sustained example of the genre. His fictitious letters are written in hexameters and take as their subject the question of the right way to live. (The second book of letters is known as the *Ars poetica* or *Art of Poetry*; it will be discussed later.) Ovid also wrote verse letters: the *Tristia* (A.D. 9–12) or *Sorrows* was written after Augustus sent Ovid into exile for an offense unknown to us. In these verse letters Ovid details the misery of living in a bleak backwater on the Black Sea, defends his life and work, and lobbies for his return to Rome. From the same experience come his *Epistulae ex Ponto* (*Letters from the Black Sea*), which treat the same themes.

The surviving body of Latin poetry was the vehicle for the transmission of the Greek tradition to European literature, as knowledge of Greek and many Greek texts themselves were lost for centuries. But Latin poetry consisted of much more than the imitation of Greek models. In the hands of poets like Virgil, Horace, Catullus, and Ovid, Hellenistic influences were transformed into something distinctly Roman, just as Europe would take the Greco-Roman literary heritage and out of it create a wholly new literary tradition.

DRAMA

PERHAPS THE MOST influential art forms invented by the Greeks have been **tragedy** and **comedy**, which originated in

Athens around the late sixth century B.C. In that city both were produced as events in civic religious festivals, tragedy at the City Dionysia in the spring, and comedy at the Lenaea in winter, though tragedies were produced at the latter festival as well. Eventually dramatic festivals inspired by the Athenian model were held all over ancient Greece.

As a civic-religious ritual, Athenian drama was literally "political," the business of the polis or city-state, which oversaw and managed the production of the plays performed in an open-air theater on the slope of the Acropolis before some fifteen thousand citizens, whose elected representatives chose the prizewinners. Hence, tragedy confronted issues important to the whole community. It raised questions about the fundamental conditions and limitations of human existence and the conflicted relationship of individuals and the state, the family and political power, passion and reason and law. It is important to note as well that the playwrights enjoyed a remarkable freedom of subject matter and theme, which resulted in drama being an important vehicle of political criticism and commentary.

As an art form **tragedy** combined the grandeur of epic's towering heroes and gods with the music, dance, and complex metrical patterns of choral lyric. Typically, each of the three playwrights chosen to compete would produce three tragedies and a "satyr" play, a sort of comic-obscene interlude centered on the adventures of satyrs—lusty woodland wildmen addicted to sex and wine—and their father Silenus. In the early fifth century the three tragedies themselves formed a trilogy tracing a single story. Later, the three plays told independent stories. After the production, a panel of ten citizens would award first, second, and third prizes. The communal importance of tragedy can also be seen in the chorus, which frequently functions as the audience's representative on stage, both in its reaction to and commentary on the action and in its interactions with the characters.

Reading a Greek tragedy silently in translation captures only part of what an ancient Athenian must have experienced as he sat in the open air and heard the singing of the choral odes, watched the intricate choreography of the dances, and admired the expensive costumes, the actors' masks, and the painted scenery. But even in translation, and even after twenty-five centuries, the power of tragic themes and characters can still move us. For the Greeks this experience would have been civic and political, a collective confrontation with the primal contradictions and problems of human existence that, in Aristotle's famous description, aroused the emotions of pity and fear in order to purge them ("catharsis") and keep them from festering within the body politic.

The earliest tragedian whose work survives intact is **Aeschylus** (c. 525–456 B.C.), who composed between seventy and ninety tragedies and won first prize thirteen times. Seven of his tragedies have survived,[4] along with fragments of others. In Aeschylus's plays, terrible suffering results from a human nature driven by its passions and appetites into arrogance and excess ("hubris"), which bring down the retributive justice of the gods. This is the tragic vision: we live in a world defined by absolute limits that we attempt to transcend only at our peril. Yet Aeschylus also sees hope in the community and its political values, which can create a more stable order and minimize the disorder created by the passions. In the *Oresteia* (458 B.C.), the only surviving complete trilogy from Greek tragedy, Aeschylus traces the

---

AESCHYLUS (525–456 B.C.) was an Athenian playwright who fought at the Battle of Marathon (490) and probably also at Salamis (480). His first tragedy was produced in 499, and the first of his thirteen victorious plays was produced in 484; his last production was the *Oresteia* in 458. He died in Sicily. His self-composed epitaph ignored his numerous plays, as many as ninety, and mentioned only that he had fought the Persians at Marathon. Both of his sons, as well as a nephew, went on to become playwrights themselves.

development of Athenian democracy from the dark Mycenean world of domestic violence, betrayal, blood-guilt, and vengeance in the household of the king Agamemnon to the sunlit world of democratic Athens and its institutions. Here reason, language, and law settle conflict, and the snake-haired Furies of blood and guilt have been subordinated to Athena, goddess of wisdom and the city that bears her name.

The next tragic poet whose work has survived is **Sophocles** (c. 496–406 B.C.), who wrote more than 120 plays and won some twenty first prizes. We have seven of these plays, including perhaps the most famous of Greek tragedies, *Oedipus Turannos* or *Oedipus Rex* (date unknown), which Sigmund Freud misread spectacularly.[5] Rather than a drama of the "family romance," as Freud thought, the *Oedipus* is really about the limits of reason to acquire sure

---

Sophocles (c. 496–406 B.C.) author of more than 120 plays, won his first victory in 468. He thus competed against both Aeschylus and Euripides, whose death in 406 Sophocles marked by dressing his chorus in mourning. He won twenty victories altogether. Like Aeschylus, Sophocles participated in the political and civic life of Athens: he was treasurer in 443–42 and a general with Pericles c. 441–40. After the disaster in Sicily in 413 he was appointed as one of the ten "advisors" to deal with the crisis. He was also a priest of the cult for the hero Halon, and after his death he was himself worshiped as the hero Dexion.

knowledge in a world made uncertain by our own passions and the vagaries of time and chance. This theme is related to a representative feature of Sophocles' drama that Aristotle called "recognition" (*anagnôrisis*): that moment when the protagonist realizes he has misjudged and misunderstood reality and now must pay for his mistake in suffering. Yet Sophocles acknowledges that despite our limitations, the need to search out the truth of the human condition is the driving force of human life, one admirable even if it leads to disaster.

The last tragedian whose work has survived is **Euripides** (c. 480s–407/6 B.C.). He wrote about ninety plays, nineteen of which have come down to us (though a few of these might not actually be by Euripides).[6] Substantial fragments of nine other plays have survived as well. Euripides won only four victories, but later he became the most popular of the fifth-century tragedians. Euripides is thought of today as more of a "realist" than Aeschylus or Sophocles; the way in which he explores the darker psychological complexities of characters buffeted by their passions and desires makes him, and them, more accessible to us moderns. He is particularly interested, in characters like Phaedra from the *Hippolytus* or Medea from the play of that name, in the destructive effects of sexual passion on the psyche. His plays detailing the ravaging effects of war, such as the *Trojan Women* and the *Hecuba*, testify to the remarkable freedom dramatic artists enjoyed in Athens, as these plays were produced during the Peloponnesian War with Sparta and were intended as pointed commentaries on Athens's sometimes brutal behavior during that conflict.

In addition to these thirty-three tragedies, hundreds of fragments from many other playwrights have survived, offering a tantalizing glimpse into a dramatic world of which we know only a fraction. But even in the small remnant that has survived we are faced with a remarkable artistic achievement the influences of which are immeasurable.

With **comedy**, the accident of survival has left us even less than what we have from the tragedians: only eleven

---

Euripides (c. 480s–407/6 B.C.) saw his first play produced in 455, one year after the death of Aeschylus. He won his first victory in 441, and his last play, the *Bacchae*, won a posthumous victory. He was not as popular as Aeschylus and Sophocles, winning only four times out of some ninety productions. He left Athens for Macedon, where he wrote a play about the ancestor of the king Archelaus and eventually died. There is no evidence that he left Athens out of bitterness at his lack of success in tragic competition. At any rate, Euripides was very popular outside of Athens—it is said that the Athenians who escaped the disaster at Syracuse were allowed to live if they could recite from the tragedies of Euripides.

plays from one dramatist have survived, though numerous fragments of others are also extant. The plays of **Aristophanes** (c. 450–c. 386 B.C.) come at the end of what is known as "old comedy," a term used to distinguish the genre from its later evolution.[7] In Aristophanes' comedies the political dimension of ancient drama is most obvious, for the fantastic plots, gross humor, obscenity, parody, satire, and outsized characters are all written with the explicit intention of commenting on and criticizing the Athenian democracy and its politicians, leaders, and philosophers, who are named and pilloried on stage in full view of their fellow citizens.

In his comedies, Aristophanes shows how the passions and appetites of humans, particularly the sexual, can be powerful forces of social and political disorder, and so require greater supervision and control than that provided by radical democracy. Yet like Athenian democracy, his comedies are in some senses egalitarian, in that he presents all humans, regardless of their wealth or rank or prestige, as subject to the same limitations and weaknesses. At the same time, we can detect in his invective a grudging admiration for the vitality and variety of human nature and its instinct for freedom and self-assertion. The subversive nature of

Aristophanes' comedy is perhaps most obvious in the *Lysistrata*, in which the Greek women go on a sex-strike to force their husbands to end the war between Athens and Sparta. By play's end, every Greek male prejudice about women—that they can't control their sexual appetites or act politically, for example—has been turned on its head, for the men, not the women, give in to sexual desire, the war ends, and the women's political plot triumphs.

The last two plays of Aristophanes, the *Wealth* and the *Women at Assembly*, are considered to be early examples of "middle comedy," a new style of comic drama that predominated during the fourth century B.C. Since no other examples from some eight hundred plays have survived, it is difficult to pin down precisely what characterized middle comedy. Judging by Aristophanes' last two plays, it seems that the role of the chorus was lessened and songs written specifically for it were eliminated. Ancient evidence also suggests that political commentary was reduced as well, as was the obscene language. Later, these comedies treated everyday people and situations, including romantic intrigue and the machinations of various con men.

From the genre of "new comedy," which dominated the third century, we are fortunate to have one play, the

Dyskolos or *Grumpy Old Man*, and substantial portions of several others by **Menander** (c. 344–292 B.C.), who wrote around one hundred comedies. In Menander's plays the political criticism, obscenity, and fantastic plots have disappeared, and the chorus performs only between the acts. His plots involve the adventures of various stock characters such as the boastful soldier, the parasite, the misanthrope, the clever slave, and the handsome but slow-witted young man in love. Most stories revolve around romance, mistaken identity, lost treasure, and various "blocking characters" that try to keep the young man from the girl he loves. But of course love triumphs in the end and the boy gets the girl, just as in our own cinematic romantic comedies, which Menander's plays resemble.

Drama in ancient Rome was strongly influenced by Greek models, which nonetheless fused with native theatrical traditions. No Latin tragedies have survived apart from fragments, including those from the plays of **Pacuvius** (220–c. 130 B.C.) and **Accius** (170–c. 86 B.C.), both of whom dramatized incidents and figures from Roman history and adapted stories from Greek myth. The nine tragedies of the younger **Seneca** (c. 4 B.C.–A.D 65.), the Stoic philosopher and tutor of Nero, are more literary than theatrical, indebted as much to earlier Roman poetry as to Greek tragedy. Their most striking feature is an extravagant violence that later influenced European Renaissance theater, as can be seen in the plays of Shakespeare, Marlow, and Ben Jonson.

The only Latin comedies to survive are the twenty plays of **Plautus** (c. 250–184 B.C.) and the six of **Terence** (b. 193 or 183–159 B.C.). These were adaptations of Greek new comedy, livened up with scenes and gags designed to appeal to a Roman audience. Like their Greek models, these plays

---

SENECA THE YOUNGER (LUCIUS ANNAEUS SENECA, c. 4 B.C.–A.D. 65) came from a wealthy equestrian family from northern Spain. His father was Seneca the Elder, a historian and rhetorician, and his nephew was the epic poet Lucan. His only son predeceased him. Seneca came to Rome as a teenager and began to study rhetoric and then philosophy with Stoic teachers and the Cynic philosopher Demetrius. After a sojourn in Egypt, he survived shipwreck on his way back to Rome, where he became a quaestor, a government official in charge of various financial duties. Seneca became one of Rome's most famous orators. According to one story, his brilliance offended the emperor Gaius and nearly cost Seneca his life. Under the emperor Claudius he was banished to Corsica for adultery. He was recalled by Nero's mother Agrippina and appointed praetor, a high official that presided over criminal courts and oversaw public games, among other duties. Agrippina also made Seneca the tutor of Nero, and he became Nero's adviser when Nero was named emperor in 54. As Nero grew into his famous degenerate character, however, Seneca's influence over Nero began to wane. Seneca eventually withdrew from public life, spending his time in philosophy and writing. In 65 he was forced to commit suicide for his alleged involvement in a conspiracy against the emperor.

involve stock characters, hidden treasure, mistaken identity, and romantic plots in which the boy gets the girl in the end. The plays of Plautus were known in the Renaissance, and his influence can be seen in works such as Shakespeare's *Comedy of Errors*, an adaptation of Plautus's *Menaechmi*, which is about twins separated at birth.

Even after the creative force of ancient drama was spent, theater continued to be an important public art form in the Greco-Roman world. Numerous festivals revived the great Athenian tragedians, much as Shakespeare continues to be staged today. Actors were organized into powerful guilds that brought theater to the farthest reaches of the Roman Empire and even beyond. Athenian tragedy thus became a force for spreading Hellenic values.

PROSE FICTION

PROSE NARRATIVE does not appear in classical literature until the first century A.D. Nine Greek novels, summaries of two others, and substantial fragments have survived, enough to give a good indication of what this genre of literature was like. A more accurate description of these works would be "romances," for there is little of the realism that we expect from the novel: that is, these works are largely devoid of the documentary detail of ordinary social and psychological life such as we can find outside our doors. Instead, the Greek romances focus on love, adventure, exotic locales, and occasionally fantasy. The typical plot centers on a good-looking boy and girl who fall in love, get separated, undergo numerous adventures and hardships such as imprisonment and shipwreck, but are finally reunited in the end. The focus on erotic attachment is reminiscent of other Hellenistic genres, such as epigram and comedy. The style is highly rhetorical, with finished speeches and descriptions of works of art, allusions to other literary works, and displays of geographical learning.

Probably the most famous and influential Greek novel is *Daphnis and Chloe* by **Longus** (second century A.D.), which combines the Greek romance with the pastoral world of Theocritus. It tells the story of two foundlings, Daphnis and Chloe, who are raised by shepherds and whose love is challenged by rivals, pirates, and the nearby world of the city and its temptations. In the end, however, even after discovering their aristocratic origins, Daphnis and Chloe return to the countryside to live as shepherds. Along the way Longus spends much time describing their sexual awakening and the charms of the rural world. Anyone familiar with Shakespeare's comedies, such as *As You Like It*, will see the influence of Longus's romance, which has been translated five hundred times since the sixteenth century.

Two works of Roman prose fiction survive: the *Golden Ass* of **Apuleius** (A.D. 125–c. 170) and portions of the *Satyrica* (more often called the *Satyricon*) of **Petronius** (first century A.D.).[8] In the *Golden Ass* a young man tells the story of how, while dabbling in magic, he is turned into a donkey and undergoes a series of adventures. There are several side stories related to the main plot; the most famous of these is the story of Cupid and Psyche. A striking development in the novel occurs when the narrator is transformed into the author.

A more significant work for the development of the novel is the surviving section of Petronius's earlier *Satyrica*, often called "Dinner at Trimalchio's." The story concerns the adventures of a homosexual couple, Encolpius and Giton. Encolpius, stricken with impotence by the sex-god Priapus, has to defend Giton against numerous rivals—a plot that seems to parody the typical situation of the Greek romance.

The Dinner at Trimalchio's is a banquet the heroes

attend at the gaudy, hideously vulgar mansion of a self-made millionaire named Trimalchio, an ex-slave. Many features of prose narrative and other Roman genres appear: complex narrative devices, side stories, erotic intrigue, parodies of Greek romance and philosophical works such as Plato's *Symposium*, and, most importantly, satire. In fact, the *Satyrica* anticipates the realist novel particularly in its documentation of social reality and its presentation of characters like Trimalchio, whose individuality transcends the broader stock types of Greek romance. At times Petronius's brutal satire of nouveau riche pretensions and moral decay brings to mind *The Great Gatsby* and the novels of a Balzac or Dickens.

LITERARY CRITICISM

THE WIDESPREAD ROLE of poetry in ancient public life ensured that thinking critically and systematically about the mechanics and purpose of poetry became an important intellectual activity. A long-lived critical concept that first appears in the work of **Plato** (c. 429–347 B.C.) is that of imitation ("mimesis"), the idea that poetry creates imitations of situations and emotions. Plato thought this was a bad thing, for he believed that witnessing certain sorts of feelings created them in the viewer and made them more acceptable. Thus art, for Plato, has a moral and practical effect, helping to create the right and wrong sorts of people through what it imitates.

The *Poetics* of **Aristotle** (384–322 B.C.) established several ideas about literature and particularly theater that would later influence the Renaissance. We have already encountered his idea that tragedy's imitation of events arouses "pity and fear" in the spectator and leads to the catharsis of these emotions. Thus, contrary to Plato, who distrusts the depiction of such emotions because they will inspire the real thing, Aristotle sees a therapeutic value in the arousal and vicarious discharge of these emotions. Other important ideas from the *Poetics* include that of *harmatia*, the tragic flaw or error that inflicts a reversal ("peripeteia") of fortune on a basically good person, and Aristotle's proposition that poetry is more philosophical than history, since the former is more universal and treats of things that could be rather than merely those things that are.

Another Greek treatise of lasting influence is *On the Sublime,* which is attributed to **Longinus** (c. first century A.D.). Longinus goes beyond the discussion of mechanical correctness in writing to explore the "sublime," the experience of delight and awe that overcomes a reader in the presence of genius. Thus Longinus gives its due to the emotional experience of literary beauty, which he illustrates with analyses of passages of Greek poetry and prose. After the publication of a French translation of Longinus's work by Nicolas Despréaux-Boileau in the seventeenth century, the sublime became an important concept both in literary appreciation and in philosophy.

Perhaps the most influential work of ancient literary criticism is the *Ars poetica* of Horace, a verse letter addressed to two brothers named Piso. In this poem Horace sets out with wit and charm the rules for good poetry. That a poem must be a unified whole, its language appropriate to its theme, and its style suited to its subject matter are just a few of Horace's rules that influenced later poets such as Alexander Pope. The influence of the *Ars poetica* can be seen in the many now-famous terms and phrases it contains: the "purple patch," a phrase that is unnecessarily florid; *in medias res*, the need to start a story in the "middle" rather than all the way back at the beginning; "even Homer nods," the acknowledgment that even a master will sometimes make a mistake; and most importantly, the idea that literature should "delight and instruct," that is, please us aesthetically as well as provide philosophical or moral insight.

Unfortunately, we have only a small portion of all the literary scholarship that flourished in the ancient world. We can only imagine the value of lost works like Aristotle's treatise on comedy, Eratosthenes' work on the same subject, or the Epicurean Philodemus's *On Poems*, to mention a few. And we should note as well the many scholars and grammarians who studied literary texts, most of whose work is lost or survives only in fragments. These scholars tried to establish correct texts, compiled bibliographies and dictionaries, produced commentaries on authors, and devised principles of interpretation.[9] But enough ancient literary criticism and scholarship has survived to indicate that among the ancients the study of literature and language was a complex and sophisticated discipline, one that set the terms for the subsequent study of literature in Western culture.

ORATORY AND RHETORIC

FORMAL PUBLIC SPEECH was an integral part of ancient political, artistic, and religious life. As we have seen, poetry of all sorts was usually experienced as a public performance.

Political activity required public speeches delivered before bodies of fellow citizens in councils and assemblies. Trials and lawsuits were for the most part competitions between speeches delivered before several hundred jurymen, and those who could afford them hired professional speechwriters ("logographers"). The ability to speak persuasively thus was the sine qua non of a public career, and rhetoric, the formal study of the techniques and skills for doing so, was the object of intense study.

Numerous orations from the ancient world have survived, giving us an important window into the political, diplomatic, and social lives of the ancients.[10] An influential set of Greek orations (including three called *Philippics*) comes to us from **Demosthenes** (384–322 B.C.), who tried to rally the Greek city-states against the rising power and ambition of Philip, the king of Macedon and father of Alexander the Great. These speeches became models for all those defenders of liberty who through the centuries have tried to warn and prepare their countrymen against the machinations of a despot whose ascendancy depended on the complacency or corruption of his victims.

Although less well known than the political speeches, those composed for court cases offer equally valuable information about daily life in ancient Greece, including such topics as inheritance, property, citizenship, marriage, adultery, and homosexuality. For example, a speech attributed to Demosthenes called *Against Neaira*, about a prostitute who posed as an Athenian citizen-wife, gives us important details about the role of women as citizens and wives and the values and behaviors expected of them. So too the speech of **Lysias** (c. 458–c. 380 B.C.) called *On the Murder of Eratosthenes*, defending a man who killed his wife's lover, opens a window into the private lives and domestic behavior of ancient Athenian families.

Roman oratory is dominated by the fifty-eight surviving speeches of **Cicero** (106–43 B.C.), which illuminate for us the history, politics, and social mores of first-century B.C. Rome. Some of these orations were composed for trials, such as the famous series of speeches delivered for the prosecution of Verres, the rapacious governor of Sicily, or the defense of Caelius, a lover of Catullus's mistress Clodia, who accused Caelius of trying to poison her. From such speeches we get important insights into Roman social history and the machinery of provincial government.

Likewise Cicero's political speeches give us numerous historical details about the death of the Roman Republic, events in which Cicero played an important role both as orator and politician. From his four speeches exposing the conspiracy of Catiline (63–62 B.C.) comes the famous tag, *O tempora! O mores!* ("Oh the times, Oh the manners!"). His attacks on Marc Antony, called "Philippics" after the speeches of Demosthenes, cost Cicero his life and bequeathed to us another model of a spirited public defense of republican freedom against tyranny. The survival of Cicero's works into the Middle Ages allowed his oratory to become a critical influence on later European culture and political discourse.

Given the importance of oratory, the technical study of rhetoric was a flourishing academic discipline. The *Rhetoric* of Aristotle is the most influential of surviving Greek rhetorical studies, treating subjects such as the difference between rhetorical and philosophical arguments, the psychology of listeners and techniques for playing on their emotions, and issues of style and figurative language. Aristotle bequeathed to the West the basic divisions of rhetoric that would prevail for centuries: "invention," the selection of words to suit the issue; "disposition," the division of the subject matter and organization of the parts; "diction," including style, figurative speech, etc.; "delivery," including gestures and pronunciation; and "memory," tricks for remembering speeches, which were seldom read from a prepared text.

The premier orator of Rome, Cicero, also wrote several rhetorical treatises that have survived. A few treat the more technical aspects of oratory such as invention, but the more important *De Oratore*, *Brutus*, and *Orator* present us with a picture of the ideal orator, someone who has not just mastered the techniques of rhetoric, but is "liberally" educated, a humanist conversant with literature, philosophy, and culture. These ideals would profoundly affect the Renaissance's views on humanistic education and character.[11]

After Cicero the huge *Institutio Oratoria* (*Oratorical Training*) of **Quintilian** (A.D. 35–90s) is the most important surviving work of Roman rhetoric. Quintilian begins with the orator as a child and hence is concerned with pedagogical issues such as the proper curriculum and what makes a good schoolteacher. Along the way he provides numerous examples of Greek and Roman writing and his judgments of their worth.

LETTERS

Several kinds of letters survive from antiquity, apart from the verse letters discussed earlier. These include private and official correspondence that survived quite by chance in the sands of Egypt, public letters exchanged by cities and rulers, the collected letters of famous personages, letters used as a means of communicating with a larger audience, and fictitious letters attributed to well-known figures.

Much, of course, has not survived; the loss of Aristotle's correspondence, which was published by Artemon, is particularly unfortunate. As examples of the third category, letters designed for a larger public, we have the thirteen attributed to Plato, which detail his experiences with the Syracusan tyrants Dion and Dionysius. Though probably not actually written by Plato, the seventh one provides information about his life that is most likely accurate. The letter form was a particular favorite of philosophers who wanted to reach a larger audience. The most important surviving writings of Epicurus come to us in the form of letters. The most famous examples of letters used for speaking to a larger public are obviously those of Saint Paul written to the churches in Greece and Asia and collected in the New Testament.

From Roman literature the most important collection of letters comprises those written by Cicero to his family and friends, especially Atticus and Brutus, the assassin of

Caesar. This extensive body of correspondence includes official letters and other communications intended for a wider public, as well as more informal letters revealing priceless insights not only into Cicero's life but also into the social and domestic life of ancient Rome. The political letters date from the decades of the 50s and 40s B.C., and so provide important information about this critical period in Roman history, which saw the rise and fall of Julius Caesar and the ascendancy of Octavian, as well as the breakdown of the Republic in the civil wars that ultimately resulted in Cicero's death.

Another collection of letters with valuable historical information is the ten-volume set of letters written by **Pliny the Younger** (c. A.D. 61–c. A.D. 113.). Pliny is self-conscious about the literary qualities of his correspondence and its value as a chronicle of his times. Especially useful for historians is the tenth book, which covers the years Pliny governed the province of Bythinia-Pontus, which is now in Turkey. These letters not only give us information about the workings of provincial government but also provide the earliest description outside the New Testament of Christian worship—along with a rationale for the persecution and execution of Christians.

As did Greek philosophers, Roman thinkers used the letter as a forum for communicating their ideas. The younger Seneca popularized Stoic philosophy in his 124 *Moral Letters*. These are closer to what we would call essays and cover topics such as friendship, happiness, suicide, what constitutes the supreme good, and the fear of death. These letters also contain information about Seneca himself and his times, and so have historical as well as philosophical value. The letter on slaves, for example, offers us a glimpse of the changing attitudes about this universal institution. Seneca's advice that "the man you call slave sprang from the same seed, enjoys the same daylight, breathes like you, lives like you, dies like you" suggests that by the first century A.D. the moral basis of slavery was beginning to be questioned.[12] This tradition of casting philosophical discussion in the form of a letter, reinforced by the model of Saint Paul's letters in the New Testament, especially flourished among Christian writers.

BIOGRAPHY

STORIES ABOUT the lives of important people came in several different forms in the ancient world, from relatively accurate histories to near fictional encomia to scurrilous attacks. Poets and philosophers, because of their public presence, were popular subjects of "Lives" that portrayed a series of individuals to illustrate patterns of influence and development. Most of these works have come down to us only in fragments and quotations. The best surviving example of this style of intellectual biography is the *Lives of the Eminent Philosophers,* by **Diogenes Laertius** (third century B.C.), who probably synthesized the work of earlier biographers and compilers. Diogenes covers the major schools and philosophers from the earliest "sages" to Epicurus. Though at times Diogenes' reliability is questionable, as he depends on earlier sources who themselves often got their information second- and third-hand, his work nonetheless is invaluable for the anecdotes it preserves about famous philosophers and for the extensive quotations it provides from their works, many of which are now lost.

The works of **Xenophon** (c. 430–c. 354 B.C.) contain several different styles of biography. His *Memorabilia* records the conversations of Socrates on various topics, from friends and family to education and virtue, while at the same time providing charming anecdotes about the philosopher and his interactions with others. The *Cyropaedia* is a quasi-historical account of the founder of the Persian empire,

Cyrus the Great. Xenophon combines useful information about the Persian empire with an almost novelistic treatment of Cyrus's rise to power; he also includes long asides and dialogues about leadership. Finally, his *Agesilaus* is a naked encomium of the fourth-century Spartan king who battled both the Persians and Sparta's various Greek enemies. To Xenophon he is the paragon of all the virtues necessary in a good and great man.

The most influential biographer of the ancient world is **Plutarch** (c. A.D. 50–120). His "parallel lives" match nineteen famous Greeks and Romans whose careers were similar, including an additional four lives that stand alone. Plutarch, like Xenophon and other earlier Greek biographers, is concerned to demonstrate the development and effect of virtue and vice in the lives and characters of great men. Thus, for Plutarch the purpose of biography is not merely to provide the history of a life, but to deduce moral and ethical lessons from that history. It is thanks to Plutarch that we have so much information and so many anecdotes about the great leaders and events of antiquity (though at times his reliability can be challenged). Plutarch's influence on European culture since the Renaissance has been enormous, as can be seen in the poetry of Shakespeare, who knew Plutarch through the translation of Sir Thomas North.

The remains of Roman biography are as scanty as those of Greek biography, but what has survived gives us important information about Roman history. Famous men or their friends wrote defenses and justifications of their careers, such as the lost work of Cicero extolling the Republican martyr Cato, which Caesar answered with his *Anticato*, also now lost. An important example of this genre is the *Res Gestae* or *Achievements* of **Augustus** (63 B.C.–A.D. 14), creator of the Roman Empire, in which he defends the constitutional legality of his extraordinary power and position and the support he enjoyed among his people. Despite the obvious self-interest of Augustus's interpretation of his career, the *Res Gestae* nonetheless provides important historical details pertaining to this critical period of Roman history.

The earliest surviving Roman biographer to not merely apologize for his subjects' lives is **Cornelius Nepos** (c. 110–24 B.C.). From his *On Famous Men*, which covered four hundred lives, have survived the biographies of famous foreign leaders, along with biographies of Cato the Elder and Cicero's friend Atticus. Nepos for the most part praises his subjects and derives ethical lessons from their lives.

The justification and defense of a great man and his deeds are a consistent theme of ancient biography. Among the works of the historian **Tacitus** (c. A.D. 56–c. 118) is a laudatory biography of his father-in-law Agricola, who served as the governor of Britain from A.D. 77 or 78 to 84. Tacitus's praise of Agricola's life is developed in the context of an attack on tyranny, specifically the emperor Domitian. A spicier and more fascinating exposé of the Roman emperors, though at times an account that is highly unreliable, is the *Lives of the Caesars* by **Suetonius** (c. A.D. 70–c. 130). Suetonius also wrote a series of biographies of famous men, including poets, orators, and philosophers, but the only substantial surviving lives are those of rhetoricians and grammarians. His lives of the twelve Caesars from Julius Caesar to Domitian, however, have had a sizable impact on our perceptions of the early Roman emperors. Suetonius organizes his biographies around the subject's characteristics and accomplishments, and his narratives are illustrated with anecdotes. The biographer thus measures each emperor against the same set of expectations his Roman readers presumably held for their rulers. Suetonius is also famous for including descriptions of the sordid sexual practices and other vices of the emperors, which he exposes with relish. Suetonius provided the model for the *Historia Augusta*, a series of imperial biographies covering the years A.D. 117–284 that was composed by six different anonymous authors.[13]

Since the ancients thought that history resulted from the deeds of great men, and that these deeds in turn reflected a man's character, biography was a crucial historical genre. Accurate or not, the details of the lives of the Greeks and Romans portrayed in ancient biography have created for us much of our picture of the ancient world and its leaders. The popular conception of Cleopatra, for example, derives for the most part from Shakespeare's reworking of Plutarch's biographies of Caesar and Antony.

HISTORY

BEFORE THE GREEKS, history (from a Greek word meaning "inquiries") was little more than a chronicle, a list of achievements or events associated with a great man like the pharaoh or the king. It was the Greeks who first self-consciously recorded events and information with a view to explaining their meaning or causes rationally, systemically, and critically, that is, without reference to the gods or other supernatural forces. The earliest Greek historians, who emerged during the late sixth century B.C., were known as "logographers" or "writers of prose." The most important among them was **Hecataeus** (c. 500 B.C.). Hecataeus wrote on genealogy, mythology, and geography, but only a few fragments of his work have survived.

Because of the loss of earlier historians' work, the title of "Father of History" passes to **Herodotus** (c. 490–c. 425 B.C.), whose *Histories* sets out to record and explain the wars fought between the Greeks and Persians in 490 and 480–79 B.C. Along the way Herodotus also describes the customs, history, religions, and geography of Greece's neighbors, particularly Egypt. Although his critical powers sometimes lapse, Herodotus is noteworthy for a rational approach to the evaluation of evidence and for his desire to find meaning in events rather than just to record them. Thus he interprets the Greek victories over the Persians as partly the result of their unique cultural values, particularly their love of political freedom.

The next important Greek historian—one of the greatest historians of all time is **Thucydides** (c. 460–455–c. 399 B.C.). His *History of the Peloponnesian War* fought between Athens and Sparta during the last half of the fifth century

B.C. remains one of the most penetrating analyses of a conflict between states ever written. His concern for accuracy, his insights into human nature and political psychology, his realist's acceptance of the tragic nature of human affairs, his refusal to admit supernatural causes, and his overall fairness (though we can tell whom he admires and whom he detests) all set the standard for subsequent historical writing as a sincere, painstaking effort to get at the truth of things and so produce what Thucydides called his own work, "a possession for all time."

Thucydides' history stops abruptly a few years before the war's end. The story of those critical subsequent years is provided by Xenophon's *Hellenica*, which traces events down to 362 B.C. Though nowhere near the historian Thucydides is, Xenophon's account nonetheless provides valuable information about the period dominated by Sparta until its defeat by Thebes at Leuctra in 371 B.C. Another important work by Xenophon is his *Anabasis*, which concerns an expedition of ten thousand Greek mercenaries, including Xenophon, to fight for Cyrus, pretender to the Persian throne. After Cyrus's defeat and death, the Greeks had to make their way from deep in Persian territory to the shore of the Black Sea in order to get home. It is a rousing adventure story as well as an illustration of the strength of Greek cultural values under severe stress.

The next noteworthy Greek historian is **Polybius** (c. 200–c. 118 B.C.), who was deported to Rome after the defeat of Achaea, a league of city-states that tried to resist the Romans. In Rome Polybius became a friend of Scipio, the Roman general who would defeat Carthage. Thus, Polybius witnessed firsthand the triumph of Rome over Carthage in the Punic Wars and the rise of Roman power throughout the Mediterranean. Five books of his original forty-book history of Rome's remarkable conquest of the whole Mediterranean have survived, along with summaries and excerpts of others. Polybius's aim as a historian is to present the facts with as much accuracy as possible, which in turn demands exacting research on his part. Moreover, Polybius is concerned to explain the causes of events, particularly the decisions that themselves are the result of various factors. Polybius's discussion of the Roman "mixed constitution," which blended elements of aristocracy, oligarchy, and monarchy, was immensely influential on later political thought, especially that of the American founders.

One more historian writing in Greek who should be mentioned is **Josephus** (born c. A.D. 37–c. 100), a Jewish aristocrat who witnessed the fall of Jerusalem and wrote histories of the Jewish war and the Jewish people, including a description of the triumph celebrated in Rome after Judaea was conquered. A defender of his people and their history, Josephus is an important source of information for the decisive first century A.D.[14]

Roman history tended to focus more than did Greek history on the attempt to shape behavior and values in the present; thus, the past is presented in ways that reinforce the writer's didactic intent. This approach can be seen in the work of **Sallust** (86–35 B.C.), who wrote histories of the Catilinian conspiracy and the Roman war against the North African king Jugurtha. In both cases he reveals the corruption of the noble class and its falling away from traditional values as the cause of political and social disorder.

Many Roman historians were themselves men of action who had participated and shaped the events of their times. Most famous of these is **Julius Caesar** (100–44 B.C.), who wrote commentaries on his campaigns in Gaul (modern-day France) and his battles in the civil war against Pompey. The former commentary, despite its subtle rationalizations of Caesar's sometimes constitutionally questionable behavior, nonetheless provides valuable insights into

Roman war practices and generalship, as well as the customs, geography, and religion of the Celtic peoples inhabiting Gaul and Britain.

The moralizing purpose of history has been best expressed in the work of **Livy** (59 B.C.–A.D. 17), who wrote, "Studying history is the best medicine for a sick mind," since it offers examples of noble and fine behavior to imitate and corrupt actions to avoid. His *History of Rome from the Founding* (*Ab urbe condita*) in 142 books traced Rome's rise from a village on the Tiber to world dominion. Roughly twenty-five books survive, as do short summaries or abstracts of the others. Surviving books describe significant episodes in Roman history, such as the Carthaginian Hannibal's march through the Alps and his devastating victories that nearly destroyed Rome. Livy's purpose is to identify the morals and values that made Rome great and that, once corrupted, led to the disorder and violence of the civil wars. Many of the famous stories from Roman history that appear in later Western literature and art, such as those about Romulus and Remus, the rape of Lucretia, and Horatius's defense of a strategic bridge, are found in Livy.

The last great Roman historian is **Tacitus**, (c. A.D. 56–120) who wrote the *Histories* and the *Annals*. The *Histories* cover the years A.D. 69–96, but only four of probably fourteen books survive. The *Annals*, like Ennius's epic inspired by the public record of the year's events, covered the years A.D. 14–68—the reigns of Tiberius, Caligula, Claudius, and Nero. Roughly two-thirds of a probable sixteen books survive. Tacitus's strength is his understanding of human character, which like most ancients he considered the engine of history, and the consequences for the empire of having emperors who were corrupt or weak. Like Livy, Tacitus thought the historian's purpose was to celebrate virtue and condemn vice: "This I regard as history's highest function, to let no worthy action be uncommemorated, and to hold out the reprobation of posterity as a terror to evil words and deeds."[15] Tacitus's imperial history was continued by another Roman historian, **Ammianus Marcellinus** (A.D. 330–95), who was a Greek writing in Latin. Of the thirty-one books of his history, the last seventeen have survived.[16]

Ancient Greek and Latin historical writing marks the earliest attempt of people to understand themselves and their times through a perception of the past shaped not by divine powers or impersonal forces but by the actions, values, and characters of human beings. As such, ancient history is as much a humanistic enterprise as is ancient poetry or philosophy. It is always concerned with what Thucydides called "the human thing."

THE CLASSICAL HERITAGE

THE WORKS DISCUSSED in this brief guide are just the highest peaks of ancient literary achievement. Numerous other kinds of writing have survived that, while not of the brilliance of the best, are nonetheless important sources of information about ancient life and culture, and so are important areas of study in classics. Many ancient scholars produced compendia of other authors that we call "epitomes." These were summaries and abridgments of longer works. For many ancient authors, only epitomes of their books have survived. Various other anthologies have come down to us in which authors and quotations survive that otherwise would have been lost. The *Greek Anthology* is a collection of four thousand poems spanning a period from the seventh century B.C. to the sixth century A.D.; its loss would have left a gaping hole in our understanding of ancient Greek poetry. Likewise, many fragments of tragedy and comedy as well as other literary works are preserved in the "Selections" and "Anthology" of **Stobaeus** (early fifth century A.D.), who arranged his selections by subject matter.

In addition, there are extant works that cannot be placed within any standard category but are crammed with anecdotes and quotations from literature otherwise lost. The *Deipnosophistai* or "Scholars at Dinner" of **Athenaeus** (c. A.D. 200) contains in its fifteen books (twelve survive) a treasure trove of quotations, excerpts, and anecdotes from ancient literature. Similarly, the twenty books of the *Attic Nights* of **Aulus Gellius** (c. A.D. 130–180), a series of essays on a wide range of topics based on his reading of Greek and Latin literature, preserves much valuable information and numerous quotations. Finally, the *Moralia* of Plutarch is the title of an extensive collection of treatises on moral philosophy covering an astonishing range of topics, from "Advice to Married Couples" to "Flatterers and Friends." As well as providing illustrations of ancient values and morals, the *Moralia* influenced the essayists Francis Bacon and Montaigne, and through them shaped the modern essay. Many of these works perhaps make for tedious reading today, but for scholars they are priceless repositories of anecdotes, quotations, information, and examples of ancient habits of thought.

The literature of the Greeks and Romans is infinitely more interesting, sophisticated, and wide-ranging than any brief survey can capture. In the record of their encounters with the world, and in their analyses and depictions of human nature, the classical authors have bequeathed to us the means we still use today to express and make sense of ourselves and our experiences. To study the language, literature, and culture of the ancient Greeks and Romans is to do more than just master a discipline. It is to learn what we are, what we have been, and what we can become.

FURTHER READING

THE STATE OF THE profession of classics and the central importance of Greek and Roman civilization for Western culture are addressed in E. Christian Kopff, *The Devil Knows Latin: Why America Needs the Classical Tradition* (ISI Books, 1999); Tracy Lee Simmons, *Climbing Parnassus: A New Apologia for Greek and Latin* (ISI Books, 2002); Victor Davis Hanson and John Heath, *Who Killed Homer?: The Demise of Classical Education and the Recovery of Greek Wisdom* (Encounter Books, 2001); Victor Davis Hanson, John Heath, and Bruce S. Thornton, *Bonfire of the Humanities: Rescuing the Classics in an Impoverished Age* (ISI Books, 2001); Bruce S. Thornton, *Greek Ways: How the Greeks Created Western Civilization* (Encounter Books, 2000); and Bernard Knox, *The Oldest Dead White European Males* (Norton, 1993). Two classics of scholarship discuss the influence of Greek and Roman literature on later Western literature: Gilbert Highet, *The Classical Tradition: Greek and Roman Influences on Western Literature* (Oxford University Press, 1949); and Ernst Robert Curtius, *European Literature and the Latin Middle Ages*, trans. Willard R. Trask (Princeton University Press, 1953).

For a general overview of Greek and Roman history, culture, and literature, students should start with *The Oxford History of the Classical World*, ed. John Boardman, Jasper Griffin, and Oswyn Murray (Oxford University Press, 1983). For classical literature more specifically, see the essays in *The Cambridge History of Classical Literature* (Cambridge University Press, 1982–85). A good place to look for translations of Greek and Latin authors not listed here is in the Loeb Classical Library, published by Harvard University Press.

Greek Literature. The most accurate translations of Homer remain those by Richmond Lattimore, both of which remain in print: the *Iliad* (University of Chicago Press, 1962), and the *Odyssey* (Harper & Row, 1967). Probably the best literary translations are those by Robert Fagles: the *Iliad* (Viking, 1990) and the *Odyssey* (Viking, 1996). The introductory essay by Bernard Knox included in Fagles's translations is the best introduction to Homer available. See also Seth Schein, *The Mortal Hero: An Introduction to Homer's Iliad* (University of California Press, 1984). Hesiod and the *Homeric Hymns* have been translated by Apostolos N. Athanassakis (Johns Hopkins University Press, 1976).

For tragedy see the *Complete Greek Tragedies*, edited by Richmond Lattimore and David Grene (University of Chicago Press, 1992). Two collections of essays by Bernard Knox are invaluable for approaching Greek tragedy: *The Heroic Temper: Studies in Sophoclean Tragedy* (1964; reprint, University of California Press, 1983); and *Word and Action: Essays on the Ancient Theater* (Johns Hopkins, 1979). To get the most accurate translations of other Greek poetry the best bet is to look in the five volumes of *Greek Lyric Poetry*, ed. David A. Campbell, Loeb Classical Library (Harvard University Press, 1982–93). See also *The Greek Anthology and Other Ancient Epigrams*, trans. Peter Jay (1973; reprint, Penguin, 1981). Also useful is *Early Greek Lyric Poetry,* trans. David Mulroy (University of Michigan Press, 1999).

For Aristophanes' comedies the translations by Jeffrey Henderson for the Loeb Classical Library are dependable. Two excellent introductions to Aristophanes and comedy are Donald M. MacDowell, *Aristophanes and Athens* (Oxford University Press, 1995), and K. J. Dover, *Aristophanic Comedy* (University of California Press, 1972). For *The Voyage of the Argo* see *The Argonautika: The Story of Jason and the Quest for the Golden Fleece,* translation by Peter Green (University of California Press, 1997). Theocritus has been ably translated by Thelma Sargent, *The Idylls of Theocritus* (Norton, 1982); see the valuable study by Thomas G. Rosenmeyer, *The Green Cabinet: Theocritus and the European Pastoral Lyric* (University of California Press, 1969).

As for historians, see Herodotus's *Histories* translated by David Grene (University of Chicago Press, 1987); *The Landmark Thucydides: A Comprehensive Guide to the Peloponnesian War,* ed. Robert Strassler (The Free Press, 1996); two translations of Xenophon in the Penguin Classics, both by Rex Warner: *A History of My Times* (New York,

1978) and *The Persian Expedition* (Baltimore, 1961, 1967, 1972); and for Polybius, *The Rise of the Roman Empire*, trans. Ian Scott-Kilvert (Penguin, 1979).

English poet John Dryden's translations of *Plutarch's Lives* are still in print with the Modern Library. A nice introduction to Greek oratory, with a selection of speeches, can be found in *Greek Orations: 4th Century B.C.*, trans. W. Robert Conner (1966; reprint, Waveland Press, 1987).

Roman Literature. There are numerous translations of Catullus available, but I am fond of C. H. Sisson's *Poetry of Catullus* (Viking, 1966). More recently, David D. Mulroy provides an excellent translation with a good introduction in *The Complete Poetry of Catullus* (University of Wisconsin Press, 2002). Other solid introductions to Catullus include Kenneth Quinn, *Catullus: An Interpretation* (New York, 1973) and T. P. Wiseman, *Catullus and his World: A Reappraisal* (Cambridge University Press, 1985).

A good translation of Lucretius's *Nature of Things* is by Frank Copley (Norton, 1977).

For Virgil's *Eclogues*, see the translation by Barbara Fowler (University of North Carolina Press, 1997); for the

Georgics, see L. P. Wilkinson's translation (Penguin, 1982) and his study, *The Georgics of Virgil* (Cambridge University Press, 1969); and for the *Aeneid*, see Allen Mandelbaum's translation (Bantam, 1971). For modern work on the *Aeneid* see the essays in *Oxford Readings in Virgil's Aeneid*, ed. S. J. Harrison (Oxford University Press, 1990). An excellent reading of Virgil in the context of Homeric heroic ideals is Katherine Callen King's *Achilles: Paradigms of the War Hero from Homer to the Middle Ages* (University of California Press, 1987).

Tibullus's poetry is available in the translation of Constance Carrier, *Poems* (Indiana University Press, 1968). For an introduction to Tibullus and his poetic milieu see F. Cairns, *Tibullus: A Hellenistic Poet at Rome* (Cambridge University Press, 1979).

Propertius has been translated by J. P. McCulloch in *The Poems of Sextus Propertius* (University of California Press, 1972). See too J. P. Sullivan, *Propertius: A Critical Introduction* (Cambridge University Press, 1976).

Horace's work is available in two volumes from the University of Chicago Press: *Satires and Epistles of Horace*, trans. Smith Palmer Bovie (1959), and *The Odes and Epodes of Horace*, trans. Joseph F. Clancy (1960). A good brief introduction is *Horace*, by David Armstrong (Yale University Press, 1989).

For Ovid, see *Ovid's Amores*, trans. Guy Lee (Viking, 1968); the *Metamorphoses*, trans. Mary M. Innes (Penguin, 1955); *The Erotic Poems*, trans. Peter Green (Penguin, 1982; Green's introduction is valuable as well); and *Ovid's Fasti: Roman Holidays*, trans. Betty Rose Nagle (Indiana University Press, 1995). For a general introduction to Ovid see *Ovid*, by Sara Mack (Yale University Press, 1988).

A good selection of Martial's epigrams can be found in *Selected Epigrams*, trans. Ralph Marcellino (Bobbs-Merrill, 1968). For Juvenal see *Satires*, trans. Rolfe Humphries (Indiana University Press, 1958). And for Petronius, see William Arrowsmith, *The Satyricon* (University of Michigan Press, 1959).

As for Latin prose: Cicero's voluminous works are most accessible in the Loeb Classical Library. A good selection from his works can be found in *Selected Works*, trans. Michael Grant (Penguin, 1960). Two other influential works are *On the Good Life*, trans. Michael Grant (Penguin, 1971), and *On the Commonwealth*, trans. George Holland Sabine and Stanley Barney Smith (Bobbs-Merrill, 1929). Caesar's commentaries are available in two volumes: *The Civil War*, trans.

Jane F. Gardner (Penguin, 1967), and *The Conquest of Gaul*, trans. S. A. Handford (Penguin, 1951). The surviving books of Livy's history are available from Penguin under the titles *The Early History of Rome, The War with Hannibal, Rome and Italy,* and *Rome and the Mediterranean.* For Tacitus, see *The Complete Works of Tacitus*, trans. Alfred John Church and William Jackson Brodribb, ed. by Moses Hadas (Modern Library, 1942). Sallust's histories, translated by S. A. Handford, appear in *The Jugurthine War and the Conspiracy of Catiline* (Penguin, 1963).

NOTES

1. Latin and Greek are inflected languages, which means that nouns, pronouns, and adjectives change their form to show their grammatical function in a sentence. The term *morphology* refers to the study of these forms.
2. See Louis H. Feldman, "Financing the Colosseum," *Biblical Archaeology Review* 27.4 (2001): 20–31, 60–61.
3. In *European Literature and the Latin Middle Ages*, trans. Willard R. Trask (1948; reprint, Princeton, N.J.: Pantheon Books, 1953), 190.
4. In addition to the *Oresteia*, which comprises the *Agamemnon, Libation Bearers,* and *Eumenides*, these include the *Prometheus Bound* (c. 478 B.C.), *Seven against Thebes* (467 B.C.), the *Suppliants* (date unknown, but early in Aeschylus's career), and the *Persians* (472 B.C.), about the sea battle of Salamis (480 B.C.).

5. *Antigone, Electra, Ajax, Trachiniae* (dates unknown), *Philoctetes* (409 B.C.), and *Oedipus at Colonus* (401 B.C., produced after Sophocles' death).
6. *Alcestis* (438 B.C.), *Medea* (431 B.C.), *Hippolytus* (428 B.C.), *Andromache* (c. 426 B.C.), *Hecuba* (c. 424 B.C.), *Trojan Women* (415 B.C.), *Phoenician Women* (date unknown), *Helen* (412 B.C.), *Orestes* (408 B.C.), *Bacchae* and *Iphigeneia in Aulis* (405 B.C.), *Rhesus* (date unknown), *Electra* (date unknown), *Children of Heracles* (date unknown), *Madness of Heracles* (date unknown), *Suppliant Women* (date unknown), *Ion* (date unknown), *Iphigeneia in Tauris* (date unknown) and *Cyclops* (date unknown), a satyr play.
7. *Acharnians* (425 B.C.), *Knights* (424 B.C.), *Clouds* (423 B.C.), *Wasps* (422 B.C.), *Peace* (421 B.C.), *Birds* (414 B.C.), *Lysistrata* and *Women at the Thesmophoria* (411 B.C.), *Frogs* (405 B.C.), *Women at Assembly* (392 B.C.), and *Wealth* (388 B.C.), in addition to nearly one thousand fragments.
8. Some people consider this Petronius to be identical with the Petronius who was part of Nero's court and forced to commit suicide in A.D. 66.
9. These commentaries, explanations, and critical notes written on ancient manuscripts are called "scholia," and such scholars are known as *scholiasts.*
10. Other important Greek orators include Isaeus (c. 420–c. 340 B.C.), Isocrates (436–338 B.C.), Aeschines (c. 397–c. 322 B.C.), and Hyperides (389–322 B.C.).
11. The anonymous *Rhetorica ad Herennium* (c. 86–82 B.C.), is notable for its section on style, which gives examples of the Grand, Middle, and Plain styles.
12. Trans. Moses Hadas, in *The Stoic Philosophy of Seneca* (New York: Doubleday, 1958), 193.
13. Another surviving biography from antiquity is the *Life of Apollonius of Tyana* by Philostratus (third century A.D.). Apollonius was a holy man and wonderworker, and Philostratus's biography gives us important information about pagan religiosity. Philostratus also wrote the

Lives of the Sophists, brief descriptions of public speakers giving speeches.

14. Other surviving Greek historians include Diodorus Siculus (active c. 60–30 B.C.); Dionysius of Halicarnassus (c. 30 B.C.); Appian (c. A.D. 160); and Cassius Dio (c. A.D. 150–235) who all wrote about Roman history; and Arrian (b. A.D. 85–90), who wrote about Alexander the Great. Important historians who survive only in fragments include Ephorus (fourth century B.C.), who wrote a history of the Greek city-states in Greece and Asia Minor, and Theopompus (c. 376–c. 323 B.C.), who like Xenophon continued Thucydides' history and wrote another on Philip of Macedon.
15. *Annals* 3.65, trans. Alfred John Church and William Jackson Brodribb, in *Complete Works of Tacitus*, ed. Moses Hadas (New York: Modern Library, 1942), 137.
16. Other surviving Roman historians include Valerius Maximus (early first century A.D.), who compiled *Memorable Deeds and Sayings;* Curtius (first century A.D.), who wrote a history of Alexander; and Eutropius (fourth century A.D.), author of a ten-book survey of Roman history.

EMBARKING ON A LIFELONG PURSUIT OF KNOWLEDGE?

Take Advantage of These New Resources & a New Website

The ISI Guides to the Major Disciplines are part of the Intercollegiate Studies Institute's (ISI) **Student Self-Reliance Project**, an integrated, sequential program of educational supplements designed to guide students in making key decisions that will enable them to acquire an appreciation of the accomplishments of Western civilization.

Developed with fifteen months of detailed advice from college professors and students, these resources provide advice in course selection and guidance in actual coursework. The project elements can be used independently by students to navigate the existing university curriculum in a way that deepens their understanding of our Western intellectual heritage. As indicated below, the Project's integrated components will answer key questions at each stage of a student's education.

What are the strengths and weaknesses of the most selective schools?
Choosing the Right College directs prospective college students to the best and worst that top American colleges have to offer.

What is the essence of a liberal arts education?
A Student's Guide to Liberal Learning introduces students to the vital connection between liberal education and political liberty.

What core courses should every student take?
A Student's Guide to the Core Curriculum instructs students in building their own core curricula, utilizing electives available at virtually every university, and discusses how to identify and overcome contemporary political biases in those courses.

How can students learn from the best minds in their major fields of study?
Student Guides to the Major Disciplines introduce students to overlooked and misrepresented classics, facilitating work within their majors. Guides currently available assess the fields of literature, philosophy, U.S. history, economics, political philosophy, classics, psychology, and general history.

Which great modern thinkers are neglected?
The Library of Modern Thinkers will introduce students to great minds who have contributed to the literature of the West but are nevertheless neglected or denigrated in today's classroom. Figures in this series include Robert Nisbet, Eric Voegelin, Wilhelm Röpke, Ludwig von Mises, Michael Oakeshott, Andrew Nelson Lytle, Bertrand de Jouvenal, and others.

Check out **www.collegeguide.org** for more information and to access unparalleled resources for making the most of your college experience.

ISI is a one-stop resource for serious students of all ages. Visit **www.isi.org** or call **1-800-526-7022** to add your name to the 50,000-plus ISI membership list of teachers, students, and professors.